A different horoscope 2014
By LILIA SEVEN

A different horoscope 2014

Published on www.amazon.com

First edition, E-book version, February 2014

The year 2014 is the year of immanent justice, which sets it apart somehow from other years. It is no better nor worse than 2013, it's just different.

The cardinal cross from even the new year's night and all the other aspects, the entry of Jupiter from July in the sign of Lion, the change of domicile of the lunar nodes, Mars staying in Libra for a long period of time, Black Moon transit through three zodiac signs, will influence largely our existence, both positively and negatively.

But each aspect can always extract something good and something bad is up to us what reasonable. So it is not fair to blame the troubles planet when our heads are held velcro.

Many of us won't have ever part of such aspects in this life, for which it would be great to try to resonate only positive with what Heaven gives us.
As our behavior is more positive, the more we can meet beneficial vibrations, generated by the determining planets of the Solar system, thus achieving the necessary harmony for a happy life.

But if we continue with our actions quite foreign to these vibrations, we can obtain only the result of some collisions of negative energies, that can bring disaster in our lives, and also in the energy areas where we are on this earth, namely:
- natural disasters (earthquakes, floods, typhoons, cyclones, storms, etc.);
- economic issues with large social impact;
- illness without medical etiology;
- armed conflict;
- major climate changes.

So 2014 can be also the year of accepting of Universe gifts, unconditional, and also of the penalties attracted by our ignorance or ill-will in order to acquire them.

It is true that this year means, beyond acceptance of everything we are offered, also very much hope for those who understood the Cosmos functioning some time ago, when we were still spoiled, considering that we were just „children", by the Heavenly hierarchies. Meanwhile, considering that we grew up ... we wait!

Zodiac - Berbec

RAM

The transformation for Ram began in autumn 2012, the process assuming a long enough period of time. Not being a sign characterized by long patience, of course they started to be quite irritated after a period of blockages of all kinds, professionally, financially, emotionally, etc.

For those who understood the role of this change, the effects won't be disastrous, for those who still ask them selves questions, the blockages will not disappear, it is clear that they didn't understand that everything that comes up from Heaven must be a little helped.

If they won't give up damaging attachments related to the material, will have a very difficult year, but if they give up untill 21-st of March, things will enter on an extraordinary path.

From 22 March the Punishment in Life will enter on the House I of this sign, it will bring many karmic payments with it, but also the mistakes from this life, in about two months these natives can straighten something.

On the House VII will sit the destiny, which means that many alone rams will marry or they will find a partner, but I do mention that weddings and engagements to program them for 2015, to be more precis after 24-th of December, 2014.

Also many social relationships can fall apart this year, so take care of the spouse, or you can lose him/her. Black Moon will enter on the House of Love from 5-th of March, so..carefully!

Also those who have lawsuits pending or under investigation it's best to try to correct the mistakes they have made (either payment of debts, or reconciliation with those affected by them) because otherwise there will be no good.

It is good that those who have vices to give them up, they still have time.

Health segment is affected to some extent also this year, so attention to excesses. I hope all the tests that you have been subjected, and some still are, will not move you away from God, on the contrary, assume your life lessons and fervently believe, and thereby you will overcome hardships.

What you should do to make this period a little easier:

-Believe in God, believe, believe!

-Show much patient!

-Diminished your ego!

-Make acts of charity!

-Respect the people around you!

-You do not pronounce evil names, not even in joke!

-Try to make yourself noticed through positive gestures accompanied by an even exaggerated politeness!

-Drink herbal teas or other plants that spring up or bloom in April, the beginning of July and the second part of September!

-Eat more fruits and vegetables which ripen in July and September!

-Eat meat maximum three times a week!

-Always keep with you an icon of the Holy Mother and Child!

-Keep a cross all the time!

-In Every Tuesday bring thanks to God, giving something to someone in need (money, food, clothes)!

-Regular incense in the house with open windows!

-Put a little piece of copper to the entering in the house!

-You should also have a crucifix in your homes!

-Make at least one purifying of the house (church service/liturgy) etc.!

Zodiac - Taur

TAURUS

Taurus zodiac natives still have the opportunity for two months from now to give the patterns, possession, pride, envy and so on, otherwise immanent justice might oblige them to do so, but in this case the result is not spectacular.

Until 21-st of March, taurus natives should put their life in order. Where the relationships went with brake applied, there should be analyzed and even drastically decided to no longer perpetuate some difficult situations for everyone. But even after this date, the conflicts of all kinds of partnerships, some can enhance, others may start.

Can be involved in processes that many of them can lose them. May appear new and relentless enemies. Attention therefore of assuming errors.

Please note how you dose your energy, because you might waste it in all sorts of conflicts and to wake up exhausted.

Health in the age segment of over 65 years old can create serious problems, but not only. The column, bones in general, kidneys, heart and nervous system may lead you to a surgery situation, but regardless of the situation do not rush retirement (those who find themselves in such situations, because you are able to work).

You are well aspected on the Family House, and many Taurus persons can have children this year or just to conceive them.

They can also buy new houses, new home objects, designs, etc.. They can make profitable contracts by selling or buying a property.

Attention also to the loves that will occur in the end of the year, they are not for life, so you be cautious. Thus!

- Strongly believe in God!

-Give up pride and do not try to put your point of view by any means!

-Don't lie about feelings and others!

-Free yourself from material regrets!

-Avoid wearing coral and brown colors in April and the first half of May!

-Wear a little cross and an icon of the Our Lady!

-Eat fruits and vegetables grown in your birth country!

-Drink herbal teas grown on the farmland and pastures!

-Try to have yellow light in the house!

-Do not fall asleep during the day between the hours of 12 to 13, especially on Fridays!

-Every Friday in April do a little act of charity!

-Confess yourself, if you haven't done it ever!

-Do not drink alcohol not produced in your country!

-Always wear a small crystal with you!

-Every Friday during the period when the Sun will be in Taurus (21-st of April – 21-st of May), you will make prayers after 19 hours, with three lit candles of different colors (white, yellow, red or pink)!

-Avoid large crowds!

-Crucifix in the house, and a copper object!

Zodiac - Gemeni

GEMINI

This year, even though it debuts with an emotional imbalance, for these natives since 22-nd of March things change. Young Gemini can fall in love and even with

the right person (unlike the first two months of the year, when in their lives can occur people interested only of sexual attractions), they can get married or engaged, some may have children, and others simply can have relationships with people who are strictly emotional attracted.

It is also the year of professional change, many of them will have professionally the chance of a lifetime. Others can change their job, or benefit of advancement at work or emoluments more than expectations. Between 5-th of March and 16-th of July attention to accidents, to health (diseases can be reactivated), to relationships with brothers/sisters, parents, neighbors, and so on, they may experience a deterioration that could destroy the emotional balance and not only for Gemini.

It would be better not to make valuable acquisitions in the first half of the year, do not sign important contracts, to avoid long and tiring roads. Couple relationships also may be affected.

-Believe in God and don't search for signs and wonders anymore!

 -Take to the dustbin the pride, the vanity, passionate impulses, jealousy!

-Do not make food excesses or other type!

-Do not develop mental dialogues in sign of admonition to the people that you just don't resonate with!

-Your ideas are not always the best ones, so ... be carefull, review your behavior!

-Consume herbal teas grown in May with white and purple-blue flowers!

-Eat fruits and vegetables grown in the spring months and also in September!

-Eat old beef and poultry at least one meal a day, and unfermented dairy!

-Avoid all that is rich in minerals!

-Always wear a little cross and a crystal!

-Wednesdays make someone joy, giving something insignificant but meant to enjoy!

-Never sleep during sunset!

- Attention to the water that you drink, to come somewhat from a purified source!

-Often wear yellow-gold color!

-Hold in the house a crucifix, a piece of copper, hyssop, basil, frankincense!

- Purifying the house (church service/liturgy)!

Zodiac - Rac

CANCER

2013 for Cancers was full of bottlenecks and mishaps of any kind. The begining of this year is just a little softer, but from 5-th of March will you release some old patterns that have given you also many headaches. After leaving the Black Moon, the fortune will smile to you throughout the rest of the year. However if until 16-th of July there will be mild material problems, thereafter things will arrange till the middle of 2015.

Between 5-th of March to 16-th of July be careful on what you spend your money, because there is the risk of a waste that can create a material instability from which you can hardly recover with all the astral help that you have.

In the second part of year many of the natives can buy a new house, can renovate the old house, have children, can travel, etc. Don"t keep visitors in the long term, might cost you the peace.

Cancers that have family problems may worsen and to produce some tears, depending on everyone's destiny. Attention to the nervous system and the endocrine one, and also to the cardiovascular axis. Also give more importance to the children education.

-Believe in God and don't bend!

-Wear a little cross, crystal and icon!

-You are advantaged by the white light in your homes!

-Use many objects in silver or stainless steel!

-Avoid pottery this year!

-Consume many liquid, herbal teas collected in the morning and with small flowers!

-Wear white, gray, light blue clothes!

-Give a gift or charity every Monday from 5-th of March to 20-th of July!

-Wear jewelry with amethyst or moonstone!

-Eat foods with high water content!

-Avoid exposure to the sun!

-Avoid skin contact with chemicals!

-In each Monday of this year make the prayer after sunset with a lit candle!

-Purify your house through church service/liturgy at least once this year!

-Don't develop envy feelings!

-Keep in the house a branch of hazel, a crucifix, a piece of copper, frankincense, hyssop, basil.

Zodiac - Berbec

LION

Finally comes the good for Lions. Although there hasn't been the most affected sign in previous years, still to the Lion lacked long enough to be happy. He had something from everything, but not enough to have everything.

In professional plane you have good periode this year, are advantaged those who have exams, tests, etc., and also those who sign contracts regarding career or profession.

Between 5-th of March to 16-th of July there are less favorable aspects for drivers or even passengers on very long travels. The beautyful part comes but after 16-th of July when many lions can fall in love, families can base, can lay the foundation for profitable business, have children, may conclude favorable contracts.

Health will create problems until 26-th of November, especially on cardiovascular axis.

- Strongly believe in God!

-Do not bend anymore!

-Wear little cross and crystal!

-Wear yellow color especially during the sleep!

-Pray on Sundays after sunset with a yellow candle lit!

-Drink many fluids, especially during the summer, shrubs flower teas and herbs specific of July teas!

-Wear amber jewelry!

-Avoid walking in the middle of the day (during the zenith)!

-Avoid any conflicts (you don't know in what can degenerate)!

-You can eat all kinds of meat but not more than 100 g per day!

-Eat foods only from your birth country!

-Avoid alcoholic drinks on hot days!

-You should have in your house a crucifix, a piece of copper, hyssop, frankincense!

Zodiac - Fecioară

VIRGO

From March until the end of July virgos are in danger of being penalized for every trifle, or to receive fines for the slightest infringement of rules, not to mention the laws.

So be very careful how you prepare documents whatever the nature they will be, especially the ones drawn up until 22-nd of March. But the good part of this horoscope comes from the House of Love, where dear natives, you are good aspected. Virgos can find their own partner or if they have it, and him forgetting the taste of love, suddenly it will regain it back and will make a beautiful life to a virgin.

Take extra care to accidents, because since 22-nd of March until the end of November there is the risk, not the physical body, but regarding any repairs to your car or the other car involved in the accident, repairs that can financial destabilize you.

There is the benefit for your to invest in something, but not on very long term, to open a new and highly profitable company, etc.

You can make new friends that will help you unconditionally sometimes, but be careful not to regret later. Between the 5-th of March to 16-th of July, the health sector may be affected due to undiagnosed causes. Be careful not to take extreme measures because there is no need.

-Believe in God!

-Wear little gold or silver cross and a crystal!

-Give up pride!

-You do not own absolute truth, get used to the idea!

-Do not make any excesses!

-Eat fruits and vegetables from your birth country, but also Mediterranean!

-Moderate liquids comsume, and mostly shrubs flower teas!

-Wear light colors derived from blue and green!

-Wear jewelry with malachite and/or azurite stones!

-Use more natural cosmetics!

-Do not wash in rivers!

-Eat more than usual: potatoes, celery, carrots, black radish, and less red tomatoes and peppers!

-Confess and share your will!

-Avoid crowded shops and markets (there is the occurrence risk of agoraphobia)!

-You should have in your house a crucifix, a piece of copper, hyssop, basil, frankincense!

Zodiac - Balanță

LIBRA

Give up attachment dear Libra natives, because that can lead you to a lower vibrational stage from where you will not pick up again. Try to get money from honest work, so you can enjoy the "indifference" of

Heaven, otherwise there is the risk that He will obviously handle of you.

Many relationships will break this year, many natives who are involved in extramarital sex relationships, will be discovered and will cause rupture of marriage or deep relations. So attention amateurs of adventure.

From 5-th of March until 16-th of July you are very well aspected professionally, business, friends, children. You can develop honest business that can bring you financial peace over a long period of time.

Health will give you a little trouble if you stubborn to believe that diseases have not heard of you. Attention to accidents!

Pay attention also to friends and friendships, this segment will provide you a lot of work, trust only in your own strenghts!

-Believe in God, you are not!

-Wear a little cross!

-Drink plenty of fluids, but not energising drinks!

-Do not make excces of anxiolytic drugs, you do not need!

-Drink flavored herbal teas!

-Rest between 23 pm and 8 am.

-Eat all kind of meat, 2-3 times a week!

-Eat fruits and vegetables grown in the hills and plateau!

-Wear light colored clothing derived from blue!

-Every Friday from now until 22-nd of March share some food!

-Say the prayer on Friday after sunset with nine white candles lit!

-Frequently confess!

-Clean your house by church service/liturgy or otherwise!

-Keep in your house a crucifix, a piece of copper, hyssop, frankincense, myrrh!

SCORPION

It's time for the new in your lives. Discard everything that was bad in your life, you are able to make existential decisions.

Try to undertake everything in the law limits, do not try any circumvention because you can put yourself in great danger. Avoid adultery or anything that can cause impotence to a family that was well-established by this time, the gap will assume a long and arduous process, full of misery that will lead to a terrible hatred. Avoid any illegalities that may sue you. Browse all that can keep yourself in position of verticality.

After November 27 your career will flourish and yourself with it. Pay attention to health, the waste of energy might plant you in a hospital bed, if you have not learned anything from the lessons of life from previous years, try to use this energy in a beneficial way, not indulged in attacks on those around you and not only, avoid conflicts of any kind.

Health may worsen, especially reproductive system, endocrine and skeletal system, the abdominal area.

Be content with what you have, because you have, do not anger God.

-Truly believe in God!

-Wear a little cross!

-Consume liquids in the summer, especially mountain herbal teas!

-Avoid excessive alcoholic beverages!

-You can eat meat daily (one meal a day)!

-Wear colors derived from red, and pink during the night!

-Avoid walking on rainy days!

-Do not expose yourself to the sun in zenith!

-Wear gold and silver, and semiprecious stones as well!

-Use cosmetics close to everything is natural!

-Protect your eyes on sunny days!

-Take salt baths at least twice a week!

-Eat foods rich in minerals!

-Avoid sugar, replace it with honey!

-Keep in you house a crucifix, a piece of copper, frankincense!

Zodiac - Săgetător

SAGITTARIUS

For Sagittarius is the year of karmic resets, of release of ballast, of the interior reconstruction, of existential decisions. Starting with 22-nd of March when the lunar nodes change their residence, these natives will start again to "live", to enjoy also of the simple things which for a year and six months does not even wanted to know about them.

Given that during this period they were somehow withdrawn, will come the time of ascention of any kind, but pay attention, there will be enough obstacles, but not impassable.

In health plan, transits of this year will give you the opportunity to repair any small or big problems that your body has been physical subjected to. Everything reliance for this purpose will give sometimes spectacular results.

Financially you are good aspected between the 5-th of March 5 and 16-th of July, however carefully to what investments you make. Also the period 16-th of July – 20-th of October can be quite good. Also after 16-th of July you are advantaged on Foreign Countries Home, you can travel outside the country without any problems.

Your feelings are also disturbed since 22-nd of March until 27-th of November. Careful how you handle the conflicts appeared of nowhere in your relationship.

-Believe in God!

-Wear a little cross!

-Do not expose to sunlight!

-Drink juices in large quantities, especially after 21-st of March!

-Try to remember dreams, they can convey to you very important messages from the spiritual world!

-Wear clothes of all colors except the coral and mustard colors, especially in the lower body!

-Make sure that in your home there is at least one mirror that shows you entirely!

-Eat all types of meat, but at least every five days of each other!

-You can eat all kinds of meat, but, to five days one kind of another!

-Eat foods from your country, and also many citrus, and also red fruits and vegetables!

-Pray on Thursdays after sunset, with a red candle!

-Take care of your skin even in an exaggerated way, because it is necessary especially during 22-nd of March till 30-th of September!

-Give small gifts or alms on Thursdays!

-Honor with great piety the days dedicated to Our Lady!

-Keep in your home a crucifix, a house crystal, a piece of copper or silver, hyssop, basil, frankincense.

Zodiac - Capricorn

CAPRICORN

Also to you, Capricorns, the South Node of the Moon submited you to a series of tests during this last year and a half. Hoping that you have successfully passed them, we optimistic head to the next period especially since 5-th of March. Martian walking that for many is a real endeavor, to you is only an ambition stimulator that will cause you to make a sudden jump from the state of damaging resignation to a financial professional ascension, spiritual, etc.. Since spring is likely to occur all sorts of tempting offers regarding work, offers that can position you in places where didn't even were thinking.

It is also possible to reconfigure some relations up to 5-th of March. Many marriages not based on feelings but on its material interests, can fall apart, causing the natives of Capricorn to change home.

For those who find their half is better not legalize relationship until after 16-th of July. Also in the period 5-th of March to 20-th of May, don't make long-term investments, they will be doomed to failure. After 23-rd of December when Saturn will enter in Sagittarius, your life will change more for the better on spiritual point of view. Health - attention at cardiovascular axis, bones, liver.

-Believe in God!

-Wear little cross and a tiny talisman!

-Make outdoor exercise especially on Saturdays, but avoid sustained effort!

-Eat local food, grown and processed as natural as possible!

-Drink many root and berries teas, and also of herbs grown on clay soils!

-You can eat meat preparations and meat of any kind with many spices but no more than one meal a day!

-Avoid excesses of any kind!

-Do not travel alone, but accompanied by any stressful persons!

-Wear clothes of brown, gray, black colors and their derivatives!

-Share something every Saturday until 5-th of March!

-Avoid sleeping during lunch!

-Keep in your home a crucifix, a crystal, a piece of copper, silver, hyssop!

Zodiac - Varsator

AQUARIUS

The tranzit of Mars so damaging for other signs, is a real asset for Aquarius, he will help you on some protracted decisions maybe since years, will give you confidence in yourself, ambition to conquer something or someone, determination, courage, legality in everything you undertake, new and influential friends, verticality, consistency, etc.

However this transit does not favor Aquarius who failed or delayed exams. Attention therefore age segment of 28-32 years old.

Another segment is health that will give you reason to rejoice. Many of the natives will experience spectacular recovery, especially in the rheumatic and throughout the bone and the joint systems. You are not advantaged on surgeries nor on a large consumption of medicines, try other therapies.

The career is also well aspected, for many Aquarius will reach its peak this year. From 5-th of March until 20-th of May there may be seizures in affective plan, or marital, or otherwise, be careful how you manage it because you are not well aspected on processes house, or on justice.

Is also the year of many divorces where there is a native of Aquarius and the relationship was not what it should be. Try to be patient and to make investments starting with 23-rd of Decembrie, 2014, and all 2015 will be favorable.

Do not sell anything at a loss! Have patience!

-Believe in God with strong belief and don't try to introduce Him into concrete!

-Wear a little cross or symbols of the Our Lady!

-Make small pleasures on Sundays to needy people!

-Consume only natural drinks!

-Do not eat meat every day, it's perfect for three times a week!

-Eat fruits and vegetables rich in vitamin C, especially berries, as well as many rich in minerals!

-Do more exercise outdoors, especially in unpolluted places!

-Do breathing exercises, especially smokers!

-Avoid driving speed, you can be involved in serious traffic accidents!

-Try a dialogue with the Divinity in most unusual times of the day!

-Keep in your house a crucifix, a house crystal, a piece of copper, silver or gold, basil, hyssop, etc.

Zodiac - Peşti

PISCES

Also this year is favorable for Pisces provided that they meet out of luck and certainly not just wait... However they have a number of attempts on the Love House, if they don't manage well their relationship, they will have some spectacular reversals of situations, and they will be guilty.It will leave you with tears and a lot of suffering, in a free way, my opinion is that doesn't worth it. Stay away of adulterous, complicated relationships, because even Jupiter could not get you out of trouble.

This aspect is sweetened by 5-th of March and it's good until then, when true love will culminate, to censor even thoughts.

In health plan the onset of the year is a good one, but even better will be the period after the 16-th of July. Between 5-th of March and 16-th of July this segment is quite vitiated. Make no anesthesia, surgery etc., because you could find out that was not necessary.

Labor House is well aspected since 16-th of July, which will determine also a financial progress.

-Believe in God and don't search everywhere for Him, He is right inside yourself!

-Wear a little cross!

-Abstain in judging the people around you!

-Avoid gossip and lamentation!

-Rely on your own instinct!

-Do not travel alone, avoid situations when you can became solitary!

-Consume many liquids (tea, natural juices, water)!

-Make exercise at least an hour a day!

-Reduce stress factors, ignoring the negative comments!

-Eat meat in a balanced way!

-Eat fruits and vegetables from your birth country!

-Adjust the silicon of your body!

-Pray every Thursday and make gifts around you!

-No longer simply make concessions!

-Take salt baths at least once a week!

-Rely more on intuition!

- Keep in your house crucifix, crystal, a piece of copper, hyssop, basil, frankincense!